CHILDHOOD FEARS
AND ANXIETIES

# SYMPTOMS AND TREATMENTS OF ANXIETY DISORDERS

# CHILDHOOD FEARS AND ANXIETIES

# SYMPTOMS AND TREATMENTS OF ANXIETY DISORDERS

## H.W. POOLE

SERIES CONSULTANT
ANNE S. WALTERS, Ph.D.

Emma Pendleton Bradley Hospital

Warren Alpert Medical School of
Brown University

**MASON CREST**

Mason Crest
450 Parkway Drive, Suite D
Broomall, PA 19008
www.masoncrest.com

MTM Publishing, Inc.
435 West 23rd Street, #8C
New York, NY 10011
www.mtmpublishing.com

President: Valerie Tomaselli
Vice President, Book Development: Hilary Poole
Designer: Annemarie Redmond
Copyeditor: Peter Jaskowiak
Editorial Assistant: Leigh Eron

Series ISBN: 978-1-4222-3721-2
Hardback ISBN: 978-1-4222-3732-8
E-Book ISBN: 978-1-4222-8065-2

Library of Congress Cataloging-in-Publication Data
Names: Poole, Hilary W., author.
Title: Symptoms and treatments of anxiety disorders / by H.W. Poole; series
    consultant: Anne S. Walters, Ph.D., Emma Pendleton Bradley Hospital,
    Alpert Medical School/Brown University.
Description: Broomall, PA: Mason Crest, 2018. | Series: Childhood fears and
    anxieties | Audience: Age 12+ | Audience: Grade 7 to 8. | Includes index.
Identifiers: LCCN 2017000400 (print) | LCCN 2017006716 (ebook) | ISBN
    9781422237328 (hardback: alk. paper) | ISBN 9781422280652 (ebook)
Subjects: LCSH: Anxiety disorders—Juvenile literature. | Anxiety
    disorders—Treatment—Juvenile literature.
Classification: LCC RC531 .P663 2018 (print) | LCC RC531 (ebook) | DDC
    618.92/8522—dc23
LC record available at https://lccn.loc.gov/2017000400

Printed and bound in the United States of America.

First printing
9 8 7 6 5 4 3 2 1

# TABLE OF CONTENTS

## Key Icons to Look for:

**Words to Understand:** These words with their easy-to-understand definitions will increase the reader's understanding of the text, while building vocabulary skills.

**Sidebars:** This boxed material within the main text allows readers to build knowledge, gain insights, explore possibilities, and broaden their perspectives by weaving together additional information to provide realistic and holistic perspectives.

**Educational Videos:** Readers can view videos by scanning our QR codes, which will provide them with additional educational content to supplement the text. Examples include news coverage, moments in history, speeches, iconic sports moments, and much more.

**Text-Dependent Questions:** These questions send the reader back to the text for more careful attention to the evidence presented there.

**Research Projects:** Readers are pointed toward areas of further inquiry connected to each chapter. Suggestions are provided for projects that encourage deeper research and analysis.

**Series Glossary of Key Terms:** This back-of-the-book glossary contains terminology used throughout the series. Words found here increase the reader's ability to read and comprehend higher-level books and articles in this field.

# SERIES INTRODUCTION

Who among us does not have memories of an intense childhood fear? Fears and anxieties are a part of *every* childhood. Indeed, these fears are fodder for urban legends and campfire tales alike. And while the details of these legends and tales change over time, they generally have at their base predictable childhood terrors such as darkness, separation from caretakers, or bodily injury.

We know that fear has an evolutionary component. Infants are helpless, and, compared to other mammals, humans have a very long developmental period. Fear ensures that curious children will stay close to caretakers, making them less likely to be exposed to danger. This means that childhood fears are adaptive, making us more likely to survive, and even thrive, as a species.

Unfortunately, there comes a point when fear and anxiety cease to be useful. This is especially problematic today, for there has been a startling increase in anxiety among children and adolescents.  In fact, 25 percent of 13- to 18-year-olds now have mild to moderate anxiety, and the *median* age of onset for anxiety disorders is just 11 years old.

Why might this be? Some say that the contemporary United States is a nation preoccupied with risk, and it is certainly possible that our children are absorbing this preoccupation as well. Certainly, our exposure to potential threats has never been greater. We see graphic images via the media and have more immediate news of all forms of disaster. This can lead our children to feel more vulnerable, and it may increase the likelihood that they respond with fear. If children based their fear on the news that they see on Facebook or on TV, they would dramatically overestimate the likelihood of terrible things happening.

As parents or teachers, what do we do about fear? As in other areas of life, we provide our children with guidance and education on a daily basis. We teach them about the signs and feelings of fear. We discuss and normalize typical fear reactions, and support them in tackling difficult situations despite fear. We explain—and demonstrate by example—how to identify "negative thinking traps" and generate positive coping thoughts instead.

But to do so effectively, we might need to challenge some of our own assumptions about fear. Adults often assume that they must protect their children from fear and help them to avoid scary situations, when sometimes the best course is for the child to face the fear and conquer it. This is counterintuitive for many adults: after all, isn't it our job to reassure our children and help them feel better? Yes, of course! Except when it isn't. Sometimes they need us to help them confront their fears and move forward anyway.

That's where these volumes come in. When it comes to fear, balanced information is critical. Learning about fear as it relates to many different areas can help us to help our children remember that although you don't choose whether to be afraid, you do choose how to handle it. These volumes explore the world of childhood fears, seeking to answer important questions: How much is too much? And how can fear be positive, functioning to mobilize us in the face of danger?

Fear gives us the opportunity to step up and respond with courage and resilience. It pushes us to expand our sphere of functioning to areas that might feel unfamiliar or risky. When we are a little nervous or afraid, we tend to prepare a little more, look for more information, ask more questions—and all of this can function to help us expand the boundaries of our lives in a positive direction. So, while fear might *feel* unpleasant, there is no doubt that it can have a positive outcome.

Let's teach our children that.

—Anne Walters, Ph.D.
Chief Psychologist, Emma Pendleton Bradley Hospital
Clinical Associate Professor,
Alpert Medical School of Brown University

# CHAPTER ONE

# WHAT IS ANXIETY?

Everybody feels anxiety from time to time. But what sparks our anxiety can vary a lot. Kids might feel anxious before the first day of school or when studying for a test, while adults might feel anxiety about succeeding at their jobs or simply paying the bills. Regardless of the specific cause, anxiety usually boils down to someone being worried about what might happen in the future.

Anxiety is a fairly unpleasant emotion to experience. It is somewhat related to fear, but it's also different from fear in some key ways.

## ANXIETY VERSUS FEAR

Fear is the emotion we experience when we believe someone or something is about to hurt us. It can be caused by all kinds of things. A bully, an angry dog, a shot at the doctor's office—all these things might cause fear because we associate them with physical pain. Of course, fear doesn't require the risk of being

## WORDS TO UNDERSTAND

**irrational:** baseless; something that's not connected to reality.

**rational:** logical; something that's connected to reality.

**treatable:** describing a medical condition that can be healed.

**Stage fright is a type of anxiety that lots of people experience when they have to speak in front of an audience.**

physically hurt; there are lots of other reasons people feel afraid. If you get in trouble at school, you might feel afraid that your parents are going to punish you when you get home. Many performers feel fear (called *stage fright* or *performance anxiety*) right before a show. Some people actually enjoy being scared from time to time—that's why rollercoasters and horror movies are so popular.

Fear tends to be a fairly intense emotion, and it's usually pretty short-lived. The dog either bites you or it doesn't; your mom either yells at you or she doesn't. Either way, the moment passes, and afterward, you no longer feel afraid. Even in situations where people are afraid of an abstract thing—like death, for example—they usually can't stay in that frame of mind for very long. The human mind has an amazing capacity to set things like that aside and just get on with life.

That's how it works in theory, at least. In practice, there's this other emotion called anxiety, which can be much harder to set aside. Anxiety is an emotion that is like fear, but it's caused by uncertainty rather than a direct threat.

# MY ANGRY DOG AND YOU

Let's say you are walking past my house one day and my dog comes running out, barking and bearing her teeth. You might feel tense or upset—you're afraid because of the threat posed by my dog. Then let's say you walk by my house a week later and the dog doesn't appear. You might feel tense anyway, because you are wondering if my dog *might* appear again. That's anxiety.

Anxiety is when you feel fear but without a direct cause right in front of you. The feelings are caused by your own thoughts about what *could* happen. You might think, "the author's mean dog might come back," or "I might fail this test," or "the plane I'm on might crash." People can feel anxious about anything—it doesn't even have to be something that's likely to occur. While fear is a response to the outside world, anxiety is a response to our own thoughts and ideas. If you can think about it, you can worry about it.

Let's define fear as *feelings about an angry dog that's right in front of us*, and anxiety as *feelings about an angry dog that might or might not be there*. It might seem like anxiety is the easier problem to deal with, since it's more of an idea than a thing. But it's actually the opposite. Dealing with a real angry dog is straightforward—you get away from the dog! Problem solved. Dealing with the *idea* of an angry dog is much harder, because you can't just get away from it. The idea of an angry dog stays with you because it lives in your brain, not in the real world.

There are all kinds of things I could tell you about my dog that ought to make you feel better. For example, I could say, "Oh, she barks a lot, but she's just excited to see you." Or, "she is extremely well-trained and always obeys my commands." Or how about, "I always keep my dog chained up so she can't get out of my yard." Those are all reasonable responses.

But if you are feeling anxiety, those responses might sound pretty empty. Sure, I can tell you, "she doesn't bite," but you think to yourself, "what if she actually does, though?" I say, "she obeys commands," and you think, "but what if this one time, she doesn't?" I say, "she's chained up," and you think, "but what if the chain breaks?" And so on. My statements are rational, and they may be perfectly true, but, unfortunately, anxiety doesn't always respond to rational, true statements.

**EDUCATIONAL VIDEO**

Check out this video about the difference between fear and anxiety.

**Opposite: The difference between fear and anxiety is like the difference between an angry dog right in front of you and the idea of an angry dog.**

# WHICH IS IT?

| Everyday Anxiety | Anxiety Disorder |
| --- | --- |
| worry about actual life events (homework, an argument with a friend, and so on) | constant, nagging worry about irrational things that interferes with daily life |
| feeling self-conscious or awkward (meeting new people, giving a presentation) | avoiding social situations if at all possible |
| physical symptoms like sweating or butterflies before a big moment | similar symptoms when there is no big moment |
| realistic fear of dangerous, upsetting, or painful situation | unrealistic fear of situation that doesn't pose actual danger |
| feeling upset or having trouble sleeping soon after a terrible event | recurring flashbacks about terrible event that happened some time ago |

Source: Adapted from Anxiety and Depression Association of America (ADAA), "Which Is It?," May 2014, https://www.adaa.org/understanding-anxiety.

# WHEN ANXIETY IS A PROBLEM

Everyone experiences this kind of irrational anxiety at one time or another. But for most people, these anxieties don't stick around for very long. An anxious college student might lose sleep during exam week, for example, but then be fine again once the exams are over. For a lot of us, anxiety is an annoyance that crops up for brief periods and then fades. The anxiety-causing situation changes somehow, or the person simply gets distracted by something else. The anxiety fades away on its own, in other words.

But it's not like that for everyone. Some people experience so much anxiety that everyday life becomes really difficult. People with anxiety problems tend to have a lot of trouble sleeping and getting their work done. They miss out on time with

**Tests are a common cause of anxiety for kids and teens.**

**According to the National Institute of Mental Health, 25 percent (or 1 in 4) teens will deal with anxiety problems at some point.**

friends or other adventures, simply because they are too worried about what might go wrong. Some are too afraid to go outside at all. When this kind of severe anxiety drags on and doesn't get better for weeks and months, we would say that these people have an anxiety disorder.

There are many different kinds of anxiety disorders. These include generalized anxiety disorder, panic disorder, phobias, and post-traumatic stress disorder. Which kind of anxiety disorder a person has depends on the causes and symptoms—what bothers them, when, and what happens when they get anxious about something.

Anxiety disorders are the most common psychological issue that kids have. According to the Anxiety and Depression Association of America (ADAA), one out of every eight kids has been affected by an anxiety disorder. That means that if you don't struggle with anxiety yourself, it's likely a couple of kids in your homeroom class do. The National Institute of Mental Health (NIMH) reports that one in four American teenagers has had an anxiety disorder at some point in their lives.

The good news is that anxiety disorders are very treatable. In the rest of this book, we'll talk about the different types of anxiety disorders and what can be done to overcome them.

**RESEARCH PROJECT**

Interview friends and family members about what makes them feel anxious. Ask what they do to try and feel better. Make a list and try out their ideas the next time you feel anxious.

**TEXT-DEPENDENT QUESTIONS**

1.  What is the difference between anxiety and fear?

2.  What's the difference between typical anxiety and a disorder?

3.  If there are 24 kids in your homeroom, how many have been affected by an anxiety disorder?

# CHAPTER TWO

# ANXIETY AND ANXIETY-RELATED DISORDERS

There are many different types of anxiety disorders. But they do have a couple of things in common. First, they all involve periods of stress that don't have an *immediate* real-life cause. Also, anxiety disorders interfere with a person's ability to do regular things, whether that's studying, hanging out with friends, or simply getting a decent night's sleep. This chapter will introduce you to the different types of anxiety disorders, as well as two that are not literal anxiety disorders but are somewhat similar conditions.

## GENERALIZED ANXIETY DISORDER

One fairly common type of anxiety problem is called *generalized anxiety disorder* (GAD). According to the ADAA, there are almost 7 million diagnosed cases of GAD in the United States every year.

## WORDS TO UNDERSTAND

**agoraphobia:** extreme fear of public spaces.

**immediate:** very close or recent.

**introvert:** a person who prefers being alone.

**intrusion:** something that appears but is unwanted.

**nausea:** unpleasant feeling in your stomach like you might throw up.

**persistent:** continuing for a noticeable period.

The word *generalized* refers to the fact that people with GAD can feel anxiety about a whole range of issues. The worries could be about big things (what if my Mom dies) to small things (what if I miss the bus). People with GAD are in a fairly constant state of stress. They worry about things they can control, like studying for tests, as well as things they can't, like hurricanes and terrorist attacks. They also tend to worry about the fact that they worry too much. People with GAD have trouble controlling their worry—they can't just "not think about it."

## PHYSICAL SYMPTOMS

Although anxiety disorders are psychological in nature, they do have physical effects as well. Some of the physical symptoms of anxiety disorders include:

- upset stomach
- insomnia
- headaches
- muscle pain
- sweating
- trembling or shaking

**It's very common for people with anxiety issues to have trouble sleeping.**

It can be tricky to tell the difference between someone with GAD and someone who just has an anxious nature. That's why it's so important to be evaluated by a professional. Doctors use guidelines in a book called the *Diagnostic and Statistical Manual of Mental Disorders* (*DSM*) to make their diagnoses. The *DSM* defines GAD as persistent, strong anxiety with no specific cause that lasts six months or more. But there is no reason to suffer for six months before asking for help.

## PANIC DISORDER

At some point or another, everybody has experienced the sensation called panic. Panic is an intense form of anxiety that comes on very suddenly—like the moment your teacher collects that day's homework and you realize you left it on the kitchen table. Feelings of panic are associated with strong physical sensations, like racing heartbeat, rapid breathing, trembling, and sudden nausea.

Sometimes people have what are called *panic attacks*, which is when those physical symptoms become completely overwhelming. A true panic attack is a lot stronger than the flash of panic you might feel when you forget your homework. Panic attacks cause people to get dizzy and feel like they can't breathe. They don't tend to last too long— usually only about 10 minutes. But they can be very

**EDUCATIONAL VIDEO**

Check out this video about what's going on in your brain when you feel anxiety.

**Agoraphobia is a type of anxiety disorder that involves an intense fear of crowds and being out in public.**

scary when they occur. In fact, panic attacks can make you feel like you're about to die.

*Panic disorder* is a condition in which people have frequent panic attacks. People with panic disorder also tend to worry constantly that they *might* have a panic attack. Because they are afraid of having another attack, they tend to avoid places where attacks happened before. This can become a vicious circle, in which these people have a longer and longer list of places they're afraid to go. About a third of people with panic disorder end up developing agoraphobia, causing them to try to stay inside, away from crowds, as much as possible.

## SPECIFIC PHOBIAS

A phobia has two basic parts: it's (a) an intense fear of a very specific thing, in which (b) the fear outweighs any real danger presented by that thing. For instance, we just mentioned agoraphobia, which tends to keep people trapped in their homes. Other common phobias include the fear of heights, the fear of flying, and the fear of particular animals (dogs, spiders, snakes, and so on).

Phobias often seem unreasonable to others— *selenophobia* is the fear of the moon, for example, while *botanophobia* is the fear of plants. But phobias are very real to the people who experience them. (So much so that there's an entire other book in this set, called *Phobias*, that explains them and discusses what to do if you have one.)

## SOCIAL ANXIETY

*Social anxiety disorder* (also called *social phobia*) involves intense fear of what are called *performance situations*. A performance situation isn't just when you have to perform in front of a crowd (although it can involve that); it could be any situation in which you might be judged. Answering a question in class could be considered a performance situation, as could having a conversation with someone you don't know well.

Some people are natural introverts, and there's nothing wrong with that. There's nothing wrong with being a little shy, either. But people with social anxiety disorder are much more than shy. They find social interactions intensely scary and uncomfortable, and they will do just about anything to avoid them. As many as 15 million Americans experience social anxiety every year. (For much more information on social anxiety, see the book *Social Fears* in this set.)

**Kids with social phobia may be too anxious to participate in class.**

# POST-TRAUMATIC STRESS DISORDER

Anxiety disorders involve intense anxiety that either is out of proportion to the threat (like phobias) or springs from no clear threat at all (GAD). But there is another disorder that's often discussed alongside anxiety disorders, and it does have a clear cause: trauma.

The word *trauma* comes to us from ancient Greek. It literally means "wound." A trauma can be

**Although PTSD is associated with veterans, anyone who has experienced a severe trauma can develop it.**

## RESEARCH PROJECT

Choose one type of anxiety disorder from this chapter and find out more about it. What services are available at your school or in your community to help people with this disorder? Make a pamphlet or poster that lets people know how they can get assistance.

any very disturbing experience—people experience trauma during wartime, or due to violent crime, terrorism, and abuse, to name just a few causes. In addition to referring to the terrible event itself, the word *trauma* is also used to describe the emotions that follow the event: a particularly strong combination of shock, anger, and fear.

Post-traumatic stress disorder (PTSD) is a condition in which the emotional effect from trauma lasts far beyond the event itself. People with PTSD often have nightmares or flashbacks about the event— these are called intrusion symptoms. Seemingly unimportant events can be extremely upsetting to someone with PTSD, because the event (small as it may seem to you) triggers a memory of the original trauma. For instance, a veteran who was injured in a car bomb might be triggered by the smell of gasoline, because the smell reminds him or her of the bombing.

But while PTSD is strongly associated with veterans, you don't need to have fought in a war to experience it. Other traumas that can cause PTSD include violent crime, natural disasters, serious car accidents, and the sudden death of a close family member or friend.

## OBSESSIVE-COMPULSIVE DISORDER

Like PTSD, obsessive-compulsive disorder (OCD) also involves intrusive thoughts. But instead of being caused by trauma, the intrusive thoughts of OCD are not connected to a real-life event. People with OCD feel compelled to repeat certain actions, such as hand washing or arranging objects in a specific order, even though it's not clear to anyone else why these actions are necessary. Someone with OCD might have trouble sleeping because he must keep checking and rechecking that the front door is locked, or he may have a ritual that involves only being able to turn off the radio when the announcer says a positive word, not a negative one.

For a long time, OCD was considered to be a form of anxiety disorder. This makes sense, because people with OCD do spend a fair amount of time worrying. Today, however, doctors consider OCD to be a separate issue from an anxiety disorder. People with anxiety disorders do not tend to have the rituals that people with OCD tend to have. However, many of the treatments discussed in the second half of this book are also used to help people with OCD.

 **TEXT-DEPENDENT QUESTIONS**

1. What is GAD?

2. What is a panic attack?

3. Approximately how many Americans deal with social anxiety?

# CHAPTER THREE

# THERAPY

This is a little unfair, but the hardest part of treating anxiety is actually the very first step: asking for help.

As a society, we tend to praise people for being tough and independent, and we sometimes look down on people who seem "needy." We also worry that others will judge us or see us as weak. So it can be embarrassing to talk about our fears and worries—we'd prefer to pretend that we don't have any. The message from society seems to be: "Get over it, already."

There is a lot of stigma surrounding mental disorders. The situation is better than it used to be, but people still feel ashamed sometimes. It's important to remember the numbers we mentioned at the beginning of this book: one in eight kids has dealt with an anxiety disorder. In fact, anxiety issues are the most common mental health problem of kids and teens. You are not alone.

## TALK TO A DOCTOR

Although anxiety disorders are common and can be incredibly frustrating, there is good news, too. With

## WORDS TO UNDERSTAND

**diagnosis:** a doctor's assessment of a medical problem.

**distortion:** here, something that is false and misleading.

**referral:** here, when one doctor recommends a patient go see another type of doctor.

**stigma:** a sense of shame or disgrace associated with a particular state of being.

**A good place to start getting help for anxiety problems is the pediatrician's office.**

good treatment, many people start to feel better within a few months. Of course, everyone is different; sometimes people feel better even sooner than that, while other times it can take a little longer.

The first step toward treatment is to get a diagnosis. You can't decide on your own that you have an anxiety disorder. Doctors and therapists train for many years in order to figure things like that out. You won't be able to do it based on a book.

For a lot of kids, addressing an anxiety problem begins at the pediatrician's office. Even though pediatricians are mainly focused on physical health, they have training in mental health, too. A pediatrician can discuss your symptoms and help you figure out if you need treatment. Questions a doctor might ask include:

- What kinds of things do you worry about?
- Do you have trouble sleeping because of your worries?

# LOOK AFTER YOURSELF

People with anxiety disorders need to be good to themselves. This may sound simple, but when you have a mental health issue, it's easy to forget about the simple things. Keep the following in mind:

- Get enough sleep.
- Eat nutritious food, rather than junk.
- Spend time outside if you can.
- Stay away from alcohol and drugs.
- Hang out with people whose company you enjoy; get away from people who make you feel bad.
- Exercise! It doesn't matter what you do—whether it's a group sport or something solitary like running. Anything that gets your heart rate up is going to elevate your mood as well.

**Getting out into nature is a good anxiety reliever. It doesn't need to be anywhere exotic.**

- How often do you feel this way?

Your conversation may result in a referral to professional who specializes in treating kids with anxiety disorders.

# TYPES OF THERAPISTS

There are a few types of mental health professionals—the differences have to do with what type of training they have and what kind of treatments they provide. These are the main categories:

- *Psychiatrists* have attended medical school, followed by four more years of training in mental health. Because they are medical doctors in addition to being mental health specialists, psychiatrists can prescribe medications to their patients.

- *Psychologists* have doctoral degrees, but in psychology, not medicine. While they are highly trained when it comes to mental health issues, they do not prescribe medication.

- *Counselors and social workers* are also trained in mental health issues—they usually have at least one master's degree. (This is less training than a doctorate, but it's still a lot!) Counselors tend to specialize in a particular area, such as family problems, grief, or addiction. Schools frequently employ counselors.

# COGNITIVE-BEHAVIORAL THERAPY

Just as there are different types of therapists, there are also different types of therapy. You have probably seen a form of therapy in movies or TV shows: a character sits or lies down on a couch and discusses all her problems, while the therapist nods sympathetically and says things like, "How did that make you feel?" This is called *talk therapy*, and the idea is that therapists use conversation to gradually guide patients toward a better understanding of themselves.

But when it comes to anxiety disorders, a different approach is often used: cognitive-behavioral therapy (CBT). The word *cognitive* has to do with our thoughts, and *behavioral* has to with our actions. The basic idea is that our thoughts about particular situations affect how we feel and act. By changing our thought patterns, we can learn to manage anxiety, rather than letting the anxiety be in charge.

In talk therapy, psychiatrists tend to avoid telling patients what to do. But CBT is quite different: therapists actually teach skills, such as relaxation techniques. People in CBT even have "homework," where they practice their skills outside of therapy. Someone in CBT might have an assignment such as taking notes every time she feels anxious. She'll review those notes with her therapist later, to learn about what exactly triggers her anxiety.

 **EDUCATIONAL VIDEO**

Check out this animated clip about understanding CBT.

A big part of CBT involves a process called *challenging unhelpful thoughts*. Imagine there is a boy with anxiety problems, and he is very focused on the idea that he might miss the bus. He can't fall asleep at night because he can't stop thinking about what might happen. "What if my alarm clock doesn't work? If I miss the bus, I will be late for school. If I am late for school, my teacher will be so mad at me. I will never get a good grade if I am late for school." And so on.

A therapist helps the boy understand that the way he is thinking about the situation only serves to keep his anxiety going. These thoughts are called distortions or "thinking traps." For example, even though there is no reason why his alarm clock won't

**Meditation can be used as a relaxation technique to help reduce anxiety.**

# THINKING TRAPS

Therapists have figured out that there are some types of "traps" that are very common for people with anxiety. A few of them are:

- **All-or-nothing thinking.** This is when you imagine scenarios that are totally great or totally bad: for instance, if you just assume you are either the best at something or a complete failure at it.
- **Overgeneralizing.** This means you make a huge assumption about something, but with little evidence. For instance, you might think, "I am terrible at math," just because you had trouble with one assignment.
- **Fortune-telling (or predicting).** With this type of thinking, you assume you know what will happen in advance. You might think, for instance, "I will fail this test no matter how much I study."
- **Mind-reading.** Sometimes you might assume you know how other people feel when you really don't. For instance, you might think, "this person hates me," just because that person was grumpy one time.

work, the boy is assuming the worst will happen. The distortion can be replaced with more realistic thoughts, such as: "My alarm clock is set correctly, and it has gone off every other morning."

Another distortion in the boy's thoughts is the moment where he jumps from missing the bus to failing the class. Again, he is assuming the worst, also called *predicting*. A more realistic thought would be, "even if I do miss the bus, I won't fail just because I was late one time." He can also remind himself that other kids have been late to class and none of them have failed.

# WHAT'S A DIALECTIC?

Another type of CBT is called *dialectical behavior therapy* (DBT). The word *dialectic* comes from philosophy, where the term refers to a process of thinking through conflicting ideas. In DBT, the main dialectic is between *acceptance* and *change*. Those two words might seem like opposites, and yet both are real and both are important. On the one hand, we need to accept that we are doing the best we can under our given circumstances. On the other hand, we also need to try and make our lives better.

DBT focuses on a lot of practical skills. Therapists in DBT help patients set behavior targets—for example, if someone is being treated for an eating disorder, a target might simply be to eat a healthy meal. DBT is not usually used to treat anxiety, but it can work well for things like depression, drug and alcohol abuse, and eating disorders. If you are interested in learning more about DBT, you might check out this video: https://youtu.be/Stz--d17ID4.

This might sound very simple, but it is actually a very challenging process! Replacing unhelpful thoughts with helpful ones takes a lot of practice. But with some work, it can turn into a healthy habit.

# EXPOSURE THERAPY

One type of CBT is called *exposure therapy*. It is frequently used to help people who have phobias, and it can also be helpful for people with PTSD and OCD.

Imagine a woman who has a severe case of *aviophobia*, or fear of flying. She just got a job that requires a lot of travel, so she has to either overcome her phobia or get a new job. Her therapist might first teach her some coping strategies, such as deep breathing or a relaxation technique. Then, they might look at a picture of a plane and rate or talk about how the picture makes her feel. Probably not very good at first! But she keeps looking pictures of planes until the pictures no longer upset her.

Then she might read an article about flying. Again, she continues doing that until reading about flying is no longer upsetting. Then she does the same process with watching videos. Next, she goes to the airport but stays far away from the planes. Then she gets closer to the planes, then she sits on a plane but just for a minute, and so on. She repeats each step until that particular step no longer bothers her.

This process is called *desensitization*, which is just another word for "getting used to it." The person does the same thing over and over until what used to be upsetting becomes kind of boring and unimportant. Then he or she can move on to something slightly scarier and practice until that's not scary anymore, either.

## RESEARCH PROJECT

Research the types of thinking traps that are usually associated with people with anxiety disorders. Make a list of the traps and come up with a "helpful other thought" for each one. You might start your research on this page: http://youth.anxietybc.com/thinking-right-tools.

## TEXT-DEPENDENT QUESTIONS

1. What is CBT?

2. What is a distortion?

3. What is desensitization?

# CHAPTER FOUR

# MEDICATION AND OTHER TREATMENTS

There are two main methods for treating anxiety disorders: therapy, which we just covered, and medication. Studies suggest that the best results come using some of each, rather than just relying on one or the other. There are also complementary treatments, which we'll get to later in this chapter.

## MEDICATIONS

Our brains are highly active communication centers, and they rely on electrical impulses and chemicals in order to pass messages around the body. One of the chemicals that is most important when it comes to anxiety is called serotonin. Serotonin is involved in moods, appetite, and sleep. Researchers believe that a deficiency of serotonin may contribute to feelings of depression or anxiety.

 WORDS TO UNDERSTAND

biofeedback: the monitoring of bodily functions, with the goal of learning to control those functions.

complementary: here, something that goes well with something else.

serotonin: a chemical in the brain that is important in regulating moods.

**Medications can be very helpful for people with anxiety, but it's important that they are taken in consultation with a mental health professional.**

That's why the most important category of anti-anxiety medications is designed to adjust a person's serotonin levels. These drugs are called *selective serotonin reuptake inhibitors* (SSRIs). Basically, they work to increase the efficiency of serotonin in the brain. You might have heard of drugs like Prozac, Paxil, Zoloft, or Celexa—these are all SSRIs, and there are many others. There are many positive aspects of SSRIs. They are not addictive, for example, and they have been shown to be safe and effective for most people. However, there are a few downsides to consider. For one thing, they can take up to six weeks to really work, which can be tough on some patients. Also, there are some concerns that SSRIs can increase suicidal thoughts in certain (not all) people taking them.

A similar type of medication is called a *serotonin-norepinephrine reuptake inhibitor* (SNRI). SNRIs work in much the same way as SSRIs, except that they affect a different chemical, one called norepinephrine.

Another type of medication that doctors prescribe for anxiety is called *buspirone*. It also affects serotonin levels, although it does so through a different route than SSRIs do. Some people find that they experience fewer side effects with buspirone than they do with SSRIs.

Finally, a completely different class of drugs, called *benzodiazepines*, has long been used to treat anxiety. You've probably heard of Valium and Xanax—both of those are benzodiazepines. These medications affect a different brain chemical, known as gamma-aminobutyric acid (GABA). The advantage of these drugs is that they work a lot faster than SSRIs do. Unfortunately, they also have a huge disadvantage: they are addictive. For that reason, benzodiazepines are not prescribed quite as often as they were before SSRIs were invented. But sometimes doctors prescribe a benzodiazepine and an SSRI together—the first drug helps in the short term, and then it's phased out as the second one begins to take effect.

Whatever medication your doctor prescribes, it is extremely important to take it as directed. Make sure you tell your caregiver and your doctor about any side effects you might experience.

## COMPLEMENTARY THERAPY

A combination of medication and CBT can be very effective in treating anxiety disorders. But there

**EDUCATIONAL VIDEO**

Check out this video about getting help for an anxiety disorder.

# HERBAL REMEDIES

Kava is a plant that grows on some Pacific islands—places like Hawaii, Tonga, and Fiji. The plant's roots are sometimes turned into drinks or teas that, some people claim, have a relaxing effect. There are some scientific studies that support this claim; one even found that kava worked as well as some anti-anxiety medications. Unfortunately kava has a big downside, which is the potential for severe liver damage, sometimes even resulting in total liver failure.

Another popular herbal remedy for anxiety is called St. John's wort. But while some people swear by it, studies have not proven that it works any better than a placebo. The other problem is that St. John's wort can interfere with any other drugs a person might be taking—making antidepressants, birth control, and even cancer drugs less effective.

Everybody likes a quick fix: "Just take this pill and all your problems will go away!" Alas, anxiety disorders don't work like that. Be sure to talk to your doctor before adding any kind of supplement to your treatment plan.

are other things people can do that may also help. These are called complementary therapies because they complement—or go well with—traditional approaches. (They are not meant to replace traditional medicine.)

For example, yoga is both a philosophy and a practice that began in ancient India. These days, yoga is massively popular all over the world. Yoga involves stretching the body into different poses, and a lot of people do it simply for the exercise. However, yoga is a spiritual practice as well as physical one. Relaxation, breath control, and meditation are all parts of yoga;

this suggests that yoga can be helpful for people with anxiety disorders. In 2005 a small study of 24 German women found that the ones who practiced yoga for three months reduced their feelings of depression by 50 percent and their anxiety by 30 percent. Doctors at the Walter Reed Army Medical Center have started recommending yoga to returning veterans to help ease symptoms of PTSD.

Another complementary therapy is called biofeedback. In biofeedback, a device is used to monitor physical reactions like heart rate, skin temperature, and blood pressure. The idea is that if you have a better understanding of how your body responds to anxiety, you will be able to use your thoughts to control those responses. In other words, biofeedback is intended to gather information in order to help the mind gain a better control over the body. In 2014, three separate (although small) studies found that biofeedback reduced the symptoms of people with PTSD.

**RESEARCH PROJECT**

Find out more about relaxation techniques such as muscle relaxation, deep breathing, and meditation. Try some of the techniques and write about how you felt before and after you did them.

**TEXT-DEPENDENT QUESTIONS**

1. What is serotonin?

2. How might yoga help someone with anxiety?

3. What is biofeedback?

# FURTHER READING

AnxietyBC. "Thinking Right Tools." http://youth.anxietybc.com/
thinking-right-tools.

Bourne, Edmund. *The Anxiety and Phobia Workbook.* 6th ed. Oakland, CA:
New Harbinger, 2015.

Munroe, Erin A. *The Anxiety Workbook for Girls.* Minneapolis, MN: Fairview
Press, 2010.

National Institute of Mental Health. "Generalized Anxiety Disorder: When
Worry Gets Out of Control." https://www.nimh.nih.gov/health/publications/
generalized-anxiety-disorder-gad/index.shtml.

Poole, H.W. *Anxiety Disorders.* Broomall, PA: Mason Crest, 2016.

TeensHealth. "Anxiety Disorders." http://kidshealth.org/en/teens/anxiety.html.

West Virginia University Students' Center of Health. "CBT
Strategies for Anxiety Relief." http://well.wvu.edu/articles/
cbt_strategies_for_anxiety_relief.

## EDUCATIONAL VIDEOS

Chapter One: Life Noggin. "Fear vs. Anxiety." https://youtu.be/aTqcgiCWu-o.

Chapter Two: Life Noggin. "The Science of Anxiety." https://youtu.
be/Z_jkNmj5S0s.

Chapter Three: Mind. "What Is CBT? Making Sense of Cognitive Behavioral
Therapy." https://youtu.be/9c_Bv_FBE-c.

Chapter Three (sidebar): UC San Francisco. "What Is Dialectical Behavior
Therapy for Adolescents?" https://youtu.be/Stz--d17ID4.

Chapter Four: Crash Course. "Getting Help—Psychotherapy." https://youtu.
be/6nEL44QkL9w.

# SERIES GLOSSARY

**adaptive:** a helpful response to a particular situation.

**bias:** a feeling against a particular thing or idea.

**biofeedback:** monitoring of bodily functions with the goal of learning to control those functions.

**cognitive:** relating to the brain and thought.

**comorbid:** when one illness or disorder is present alongside another one.

**context:** the larger situation in which an event takes place.

**diagnose:** to identify an illness or disorder.

**exposure:** having contact with something.

**extrovert:** a person who enjoys being with others.

**harassment:** picking on another person frequently and deliberately.

**hypnosis:** creating a state of consciousness where someone is awake but highly open to suggestion.

**inhibitions:** feelings that restricts what we do or say.

**introvert:** a person who prefers being alone.

**irrational:** baseless; something that's not connected to reality.

**melatonin:** a substance that helps the body regulate sleep.

**milestone:** an event that marks a stage in development.

**motivating:** something that makes you want to work harder.

**occasional:** from time to time; not often.

**panic attack:** sudden episode of intense, overwhelming fear.

**paralyzing:** something that makes you unable to move (can refer to physical movement as well as emotions).

peers: people who are roughly the same age as you.

perception: what we see and believe to be true.

persistent: continuing for a noticeable period.

phobia: extreme fear of a particular thing.

preventive: keeping something from happening.

probability: the likelihood that a particular thing will happen.

psychological: having to do with the mind and thoughts.

rational: based on a calm understanding of facts, rather than emotion.

sedative: a type of drug that slows down bodily processes, making people feel relaxed or even sleepy.

self-conscious: overly aware of yourself, to the point that it makes you awkward.

serotonin: a chemical in the brain that is important in moods.

stereotype: an oversimplified idea about a type of person that may not be true for any given individual.

stigma: a sense of shame or disgrace associated with a particular state of being.

stimulant: a group of substances that speed up bodily processes.

subconscious: thoughts and feelings you have but may not be aware of.

syndrome: a condition.

treatable: describes a medical condition that can be healed.

upheaval: a period of great change or uncertainty.

# INDEX

# ABOUT THE ADVISOR

**Anne S. Walters** is Clinical Associate Professor of Psychiatry and Human Behavior at the Alpert Medical School of Brown University. She is also Chief Psychologist for Bradley Hospital. She is actively involved in teaching activities within the Clinical Psychology Training Programs of the Alpert Medical School and serves as Child Track Seminar Co-Coordinator. Dr. Walters completed her undergraduate work at Duke University, graduate school at Georgia State University, internship at UTexas Health Science Center, and postdoctoral fellowship at Brown University.

# ABOUT THE AUTHOR

**H. W. Poole** is a writer and editor of books for young people, including the sets, *Families Today* and *Mental Illnesses and Disorders: Awareness and Understanding* (Mason Crest). She created the *Horrors of History* series (Charlesbridge) and the *Ecosystems* series (Facts On File). She has also been responsible for many critically acclaimed reference books, including *Political Handbook of the World* (CQ Press) and the *Encyclopedia of Terrorism* (SAGE). She was coauthor and editor of *The History of the Internet* (ABC-CLIO), which won the 2000 American Library Association RUSA award.

# PHOTO CREDITS